Would you like to see the house?

Would you like to see the house?

Unapologetic interiors filled with color, verve, oh and there's a door on the ceiling!

— Lorraine Kirke

Photography by PATTI STOECKER

RIZZOLI
NEW YORK

New York · Paris · London · Milan

Lorraine Kirke's style is part New Orleans brothel, part upper-crust teatime, and all her own. Her spaces are like theater sets—endless secrets to discover, incredible attention to character, and there's a dramatic nook for every occasion. As soon as you enter a Lorraine Kirke space you will never want to leave, you will feel like a different person, and you will know Lorraine intimately. That is her gift.

—Lena Dunham

Contents

Preface

Lorraine and I were a match waiting to happen. One day she rang me up in Miami because she'd heard about the vintage dresses I sold and so our friendship began.

The idea to photograph her gorgeous over-the-top West Village town house for a book took all of five minutes, after she gave me the tour of the house.

Lorraine's talent is completely unique. She has no limits. She'll do anything. She's absolutely fearless about moving things around and changing things up. When she loves something it's not about how much it costs; she'll hang a dollar painting next to a Picabia. Lorraine expresses herself completely honestly—she can't help it!

With so many signature traits, it's hard to say what my favorites are but I'll give it a go: the cozy nooks; the massive amounts of fabric; the dyed crocheted lace drapes; vintage lamps with beads and fringes everywhere; black painted trim outlining doors and windows; antiques mixed with fun flea market finds; color, color, and more color—and when a particular color doesn't suit her, there's always a can of spray paint waiting in the wings.

—Patti Stoecker

Introduction

Why is your taste so ridiculously good?
How did you get it?
Can I have some?
And why does it all seem to be so maddeningly effortless?

You're part collector, part conjurer, part magnet for beautiful things. We go places where ninety-nine percent of everything is not worth looking at and somehow all the beautiful things have attached themselves to you by the time we leave. It's like they wait to be found by you. Furniture, fabrics, treasures, all of it. And then you do your conjuring and everything looks like it's belonged together forever. I think the wall in your house that you covered in old shutters makes me the most mad. So simple, so beautiful. Then there's your sense of color, like you're willing to wait for colors to mature into themselves before you're ready to use them. Weathered isn't the word, old isn't either, more like storied, like the colors you use have had a life, like they have a story. But that is you, and maybe all of us: a life and a story. All of that to say, I feel so lucky to know you, to delight in your artistry, and to see the beauty you see.

And could you please just not make it all look so easy.

—Mariska Hargitay

Foreword

It's hard not to fall under the spell of Lorraine Kirke—her houses have a glorious three dimensional effect on the senses, rather like the pages of your favorite book coming to life in front of your eyes. The colors and conviviality she conjures up seem almost from another time.

Hers were the parties that they all flocked to whether it be London, Miami or NYC. A dinner at Lorraine's is a treasured invite—so when I received an invitation to dinner, I knew it was something special. This was the house I'd literally stood outside a million times drooling over the window boxes. Strange Japanese looking tendrils of yellow and gold tumbled from the dark metal window boxes like hundreds of wayward threads of gold. Then the stoop—well that was a vision to behold. A mishmash of beautiful war-torn pots brimming with color and foliage leaving just enough room to climb the stairs to the magic that was behind that door.

As the door opened, the gasp that leaped out of my mouth before I could stop it was beyond embarrassing. The almost electric green of the banister that shocked the retinas on entering the hallway was spectacular.

Her homes are always subject to a revolving door of renovations and improvements. At her happiest, she is at her busiest and there is a never-ending carousel of changes that everyone around her takes as 'the norm.'

Entering the sitting room I was bombarded by beauty—on every level, but it didn't feel jammed to the ceiling like some places can. Everything had its place and was loved equally—nothing was hidden and every painting and photograph felt as at home as the people looking back at them. Nothing was forced, everything was at one with its surroundings.

Lorraine is a natural artist, brimming with ideas. Upon tumbling down the staircase into the basement another Alice in Wonderland grotto awaits you but it's not overwhelming—it's calming, comfortable, safe even. Nothing is sacred, pretentious or priceless.

Lorraine never ceases to amaze with her creative combinations of the unexpected. Old weathered and a little bit broken, these motley objects have one thing in common—they all have life in them.

If they could talk you know they would tell stories of the rooms they've lived in and the memories that are yet to come.

—Angela McCluskey

Each time I walk into one of Lorraine's homes, I feel a complete inadequacy in my own design capabilities—I feel drab and safe and simple. I dream of being as interesting and layered. Lorraine's homes are a true reflection of her—layered, deep, colorful, rich, storied, interesting, dark, rock'n'roll, eclectic. You can imagine a rich tapestry of life had been lived at 11th Street, and those walls could surely tell a tale or two.

—Annabel White

WEST VILLAGE TOWNHOUSE

When I first walked into the house
I wasn't sure it was really for me.
Then through the window I saw
the magnolia tree outside!

First. Time to get creative –
take down the door to the
hallway and then every other
door that gets in my way, of course
now I was left with a pile of beautiful
doors and I was not throwing them out.
So I chopped them up and panelled
the walls and ceiling.

Much better!

This chandelier used to annoy me
then I found my can of black spray paint.

I've always been inspired by Lorraine and her energy and creative force. She manages to take a space and create a bohemian, surrealist, cozy salon that you just want to stay in and never leave, filled with fabric, wood and many, many books. She's spent years living her life for others—I'm excited to see the next chapter in her life.

—Rosanna Arquette

50

50

PREVIOUS PAGE:

Hanging pictures on top of aged, distressed mirrors, where you can no longer see yourself.

Why not?

You can never have enough mirrors

PREVIOUS PAGE + OPPOSITE:

One of the first paintings I ever bought — the dress inspired my design business "Geminola" (a store in the west village) — I told my kids it was of their great great grandmother and left it at that.

15 years later Jemima said "I need to talk to you about our great great grandmother!"

The dining room chandelier was just an old thing I found at a flea market and I never had it wired, just ~~ADDED~~ candles.

People who come to dinner expect to go home with wax in their hair.

That's the price of a beautiful candelabra – It's all part of the fun.

Lorraine's gift for decoration finds its inspiration in her love of family, people, and celebration. Every interior has an enticingly comfortable place to sit, lounge, and converse. Each dress celebrates your inner eccentric and most secret self. Her meals encourage lingering and confession, and she accomplishes it all with a bold palette and a keen eye for beauty.

—Julianne Moore

BRYSON
Amis
Ireland

Lorraine really taught me how to channel my creativity—even the way she keeps her books is chic. She creates a feast for the eyes and soul. The way she moves doors, windows, and bathtubs is genius. Every fork, every teacup has thought behind it, yet one can be oneself and relax in Lorraine's amazing environments and, of course, her wonderful nooks—only Lorraine can create those. I've spent many an hour confessing my secrets in them.

—Courtney Love

DEFENSE

Along with my friend and brilliant
carpenter Tom Muchowski there was
No end of possibilities.
Old doors became walls
and walls became galleries –

FOLLOWING PAGES:

I wasn't sure what to do with this awkward space. Nothing would fit – and then we decided to cut the sofa in half

It kind of worked!

DEFENSE
DE FUME

DÉFENSE
DE FUMER

PREVIOUS PAGE:

The tin tiles on the kitchen ceiling come in all colors — I didn't have time to figure out which ones would work best when I bought them, but they turned out fine.

& sometimes it's just a jigsaw puzzle.

BREAD

The dark bordeaux color of wine
has long been a favorite.
When in doubt, that was the color
of choice –

The Hallway

If someone was in trouble or getting a divorce, our door was always open. There were a lot of sad women, and naked women, and sad naked women, and they weren't always in the paintings.

—Lola Kirke

We grew up around Mapplethorpes and really erotic pictures, and all kinds of art, the sad naked lady stuff. I liked that it was sad. Then there were flea market ones that are shit. She's not buying them because they're great paintings—she buys them as props, almost.

—Jemima Kirke

PREVIOUS PAGE:

Instead of placing the mirror on top of the fireplace, take the frame off and make it the mantel.

My mother finds beauty in things that not everyone sees as beautiful; like a tattered old painting, or a beautiful girl who has thick eyebrows. Things that others may not see. That really inspired my painting; looking for beauty in things that aren't obvious. She makes damaged goods feel at home.

—Jemima Kirke

Freud would have painted someone lounging here.

When she came to New York and she brought that Victoriana, leopard skin, art of mix and mess, I think it took NY by storm. It is quintessentially English. I like the way her house glows at night and you glow in return.

—Fiona Golfar

Maybe Sigmund would have made sense of me here.

GRACE

What I like in a dressing room? Everything — my favorite place to hang out, my "man cave."

Ok, so she was young enough at the time to put her name in mirrored chips into the concrete floor.

I mean, you can totally imagine Toulouse Lautrec walking around with a glass of Absinthe, touting a prostitute on a bench.

—Griffin Dunne

SPRINGS—

Great place to grow up, right on the bay.
I bought the house in Springs but kids don't
always see things the same way you do—
and they did not want to move.
So the first night, there we were and ~~to~~
they sat sulking in silence. I was
determined to get them to like it.
Tom helped—he was a surfer, so he'd
disappear for hours and I'd say "why were
you surfing when you were supposed to
be working?" He's just tell me "Shhh"
and then build me something incredible
out of driftwood that he'd found on the beach.

When I woke up one morning to see my
youngest daughter Lela swimming out to the dock,
I knew it had become a home.

The Kitchen

The tiniest details
make the difference —
A tin kettle or a
dripping candelabra
that's seen it all.

It's where we congregate
It's that kitchen again

I don't like upholstering, it's too permanent; finding beautiful fabrics and being able to change them out when the mood takes you is what I do. Perfection was my mother's thing.

Imperfection's mine.

I always consider both the outside & inside when dressing a room. I'm not one for staring out of windows, but I like to know I've dressed them for the occasion should I ever have a change of heart.

The Dining Room

I fell in love with her home the minute I walked in. It was truly the essence of her creativity and style and soul!

—Stacey Eisner

Wallpaper can bring an unloved corner to life. Even the tiniest of squares can evoke a glamour of another time. The nook; under the stairs; the bookshelves; on a landing; on the ceiling of a bedroom. Wallpaper can bring out the unexpected by putting it in a place where it wouldn't usually be.

Every corner
has a story –
it's not cluttered
or decaying but
it's not brand
new &
sparkly clean.

It's somewhere
in the middle
where life lives.

PREVIOUS PAGE:

Ok, you ran out of fabric so you use what you have - and that makes it original to you & sometimes it actually works.

SPRAY

The Guesthouse

I want to stay here.
perfect for that marital
squabble.

The Bathroom

Cozy Spaces Outside

Antiques are like people. If they are in your home it's because you enjoy their company.

OCEAN FRONT DUET –

When I see apartments like Jo Wood's before she bought it, all white & soulless it's not about decorating – I just feel I have to go and rescue it. Jo saw it and said "are you sure?" It really was hideous, with a built in shiny black bed, shelves & TV cabinets.

Six weeks later, here it is. It was so enjoyable working with Jo. We have similar taste & enthusiasm, so I felt like I was doing it for myself, and worked with the same excitement as if it were mine. Waking in the middle of the night thinking God, I have to move that chair tomorrow!

I've been friends with Lorraine since I was 18. She's been a big part of my life—we've been through marriages, children, homes, and now grandkids together. She's always been there for me and I have for her—I've seen all the homes she's lived in and watched her style blossom… I love the way Lorraine uses color and has no fear with bright bold colors (something I find hard to do). We've always shared a passion for vintage and antiques, and I can think of nobody else in the world I'd rather wander around flea markets and antique and junk shops with than Lorraine. She's a force to be reckoned with when doing her interiors, and she amazes me how quickly she pulls things together. She really is a bit special.

—Jo Wood

MIAMI BEACH

It was on a bike ride when we saw a "for sale" sign in a window and the next thing we knew we owned a little piece of beach paradise.

Miami was so foreign to me and I loved its kitsch side. I set about restoring the apartment to the year it was built, 1929 - No plain white condo for me.

The Lincoln road flea market became my favorite haunt. It was like being someone else. My little bit of fantasy - creating a life out there that didn't really exist for me. An escape.

It was playful, and tiny and crammed with my family - it worked!

515

A great portrait
becomes your muse.

This muse worked
wonders for me in Miami,
I became someone else.

I don't know how she figures out that X is a perfect match with J, but she is true to herself and is undaunted by the greatest challenges. I would follow her to any flea market, antique fair or strip-mall dollar store. I can't imagine having more fun watching someone turn an empty room into a space that makes you sigh with pleasure just by walking into it.

—Marie-Louise Parker

There's a lot of something very grandiose paired with something really dilapidated. I think that's how I'd describe it. Everything looks 100 years old.

—Lola Kirke

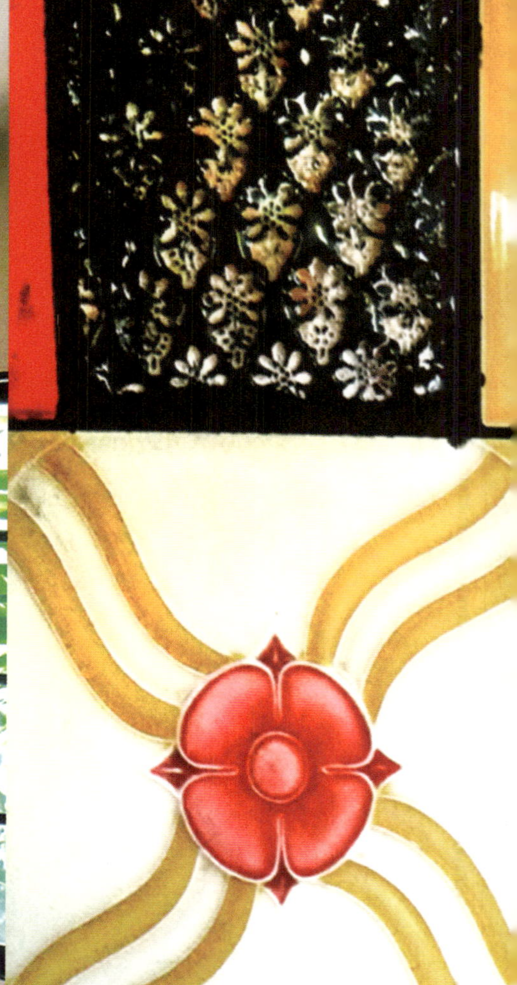

The Bedroom

outside Architectural
pieces brought inside.

DRAMA!

Fashion is a good dress. Style is living uniquely and unapologetically.
It permeates everything one does. Lorraine Kirke has style to spare.

—Carole Radziwill

Afterword

We've moved so many times but Mum was always able to make everywhere we went look like we'd been there for seventy-five years within about seven days—it's a tremendous talent. And emotionally it was very reassuring because everything always looked like home.

I don't think I've still fully processed how unique her style really is. Every person who walked into our house had a crazy reaction to it. You can't blame them, I guess.

Mum's style is very glamorous and cinematic. There was a lot of room for me to play around in and to imagine being whoever it was I wanted to be. It's a privilege to grow up in such a creative world. It gives you permission to believe that it's a totally valid avenue of living and existence. It would have been weird if we hadn't turned out creative. When I was growing up I just wanted a normal house, of course—an apartment where everything was white. In the end Mum worked with me so that my room was more Lola and less Lorraine. But I've definitely taken her influence away. I think you'd have to have bad taste not to. She has the best ideas. She's enabled me to live in a retrograde kind of way. I really believe the quality of old things is so much better—even if they are falling apart.

It wasn't all a bed of roses though. There wasn't much privacy in my mum's style. You go to other people's homes and they give very little away—it's like there's something hidden. Our houses didn't leave much to the imagination. But I also think it made us stronger people, being such an open book.

—Lola Kirke

Thank you

For her vision & amazing talent + love & friendship – PATTI Stoecker

For his time + patience – KARL Stoecker

Gorgeous tiles – Carlos Alvez

Brilliant carpenter – Thomas Muchowski

Architect who understands me and puts up with me – Richard Lewis

2nd Hand Rose – Wallpapers

Specialised painting – Robert PADILLA

To my children Gregory, Domino, Jemima & Lola – for living amongst the drama.

Geoffrey Dunne – for understanding + putting this together.

Daniel MelAMUD – for making this a book.

& finally to all my friends for their generous and loving words —

– Lorraine Kirke

It is with gratitude and all my heart that I wish to thank—

Karl Stoecker, Luke Flynn, Ken Ferdman, Kimberly Gonzalez, Sheena Stoecker, Samantha Flynn… and most appreciatively Jo Wood, Antonia Short and Geoffrey Dunne…

To Lorraine Kirke for sharing with me her gorgeous homes to photograph… and Charles Miers and Daniel Melamud at Rizzoli for embracing this book.

—Patti Stoecker

First published in the United States of America in 2016 by
Rizzoli International Publications, Inc.
300 Park Avenue South
New York, NY 10010
www.rizzoliusa.com

Editor: Daniel Melamud
Design: Geoffrey Dunne
Production: Maria Pia Gramaglia

Library of Congress Control Number: 2015953970
ISBN-13: 978-0-8478-4750-1

2016 2017 2018 2019 / 10 9 8 7 6 5 4 3 2 1
Printed in China